Cryptocurrency 1x1 The Guide to Financial Freedom

How you deeply understand blockchain, invest in cryptocurrencies and achieve maximum return incl. Bitcoin, Altcoin and More

Andrew P. Hammond

Table of Contents

Chapter 1

Understanding the Basics of Blockchain Technology & Cryptocurrencies

"Every informed person needs to know about Bitcoin because it might be one of the world's most important developments."
Leon Louw, two-time Nobel Peace Prize nominee.

Do you wonder why Leon Louw made this million-dollar statement? It's because over the last decade, a clear statement has been made. Blockchain technology and cryptocurrencies are here to take over the financial landscape.

It gets clearer and even more convincing when considering how fast the value of certain cryptocurrencies like Bitcoin and Ethereum has increased in the last two years. However, there is a lot more potential in this technology that remains undiscovered.

So, are you ready to fully understand what blockchain technology is all about? Or do you wish to invest wisely in cryptocurrencies and achieve maximum return on your Bitcoin or Altcoins investments?

If your answer is positive, then it's my pleasure to let you know that your earth auger just struck gold!

This chapter sets the tone for what will become an expository and revealing experience for you as you read through this book. In the pages of this chapter, you will be furnished with the knowledge of fundamental aspects of blockchain technology and cryptocurrencies. Not only will this chapter take off the thick clouds on many cryptocurrency terms. It will also do well to soothe your fears and refute conspiracy theories you must have heard about the technology.

A good place to begin channeling cryptocurrency as a road to financial freedom is first understanding what the bogus terminologies in the industry mean. Here's a timeless explanation of the five foundational words in cryptocurrency.

- Cryptocurrency

  Cryptocurrency is simply a virtual currency or asset, also referred to as digital money. It is a currency developed based on cryptographic sciences and computing technology.

- Bitcoin

  Bitcoin is a type of cryptocurrency developed using Blockchain technology. Bitcoin is the first well-known and widely accepted cryptocurrency.

- Blockchain Technology

  This is the technology used to develop the Bitcoin cryptocurrency. Blockchain technology counts on cryptology and the internet (peer-to-peer networking) to function.

- DeFi

  DeFi is the short form of "decentralized finance." Unlike other complex terms, this is just an umbrella name for all types of cryptocurrencies that avoid intermediaries and centralized control.

That's why no Central Bank or Federal Reserves is regulating the value of crypto assets.

- Wallet

Cryptocurrency wallets are the digital equivalents of banks. They assist cryptocurrency investors store, manage, and transfer their assets.

How It All Began And What The Future Holds

Although most people refer to Bitcoin as new, it has, in fact, existed for over a decade already. The bitcoin journey began in 2009. The bedrock technology for this cryptocurrency has, in fact, existed for a much longer period. Anyone who had taken the leap to invest $1,000 in Bitcoin in 2009, when it was first made public, would have now amassed wealth amounting to over $50 million. Sounds impossible? Then you might want to check out the story of Matthew Rosnak. He adopted Bitcoin early enough in 2011, and today, he is worth a whooping portfolio value of $1 billion. Now, that's some investment with foresight.

The next big question is, how did the journey begin for blockchain technology and cryptocurrency? In this section, I will be providing the answers you need. Come along as I walk you through the full chronicles of Bitcoin and cryptocurrency.

The Pre-Bitcoin Years (1998 – 2009)

As you might have learned, Bitcoin was the first cryptocurrency that was widely known and accepted. However, there had been prior tries at establishing online currencies with ledgers that are protected by encryption (a major feature of cryptocurrencies). Two good examples of these earlier attempts are Bit Gold and B-Money. These two were only formulated; they never truly got to the execution and public adoption stage.

The Mysterious Mr. Nakamoto (2008)

Then in 2008, something interesting happened that will forever change the narrative of fiat and digital currencies. On a mailing list discussion on cryptography, someone posted a paper referred to as Bitcoin (A Peer-to-Peer Electronic Cash System). It was later revealed that this paper was posted by a certain Satoshi Nakamoto (not his real name). And up till the point of this writing, the real identity of this individual is still unknown.

The Beginning of the Bitcoin Era (2009)

The Bitcoin software became accessible publicly for the very first time in 2009. At the same time, mining, which is the process by which new Bitcoins are developed and transactions are computed and validated on the Blockchain, started.

Bitcoin Got Its First-Ever Value (2010)

Assigning a particular monetary value to each unit of this fast-rising cryptocurrency was practically impossible. This is as Bitcoin was only mined then; it had never been traded.

In 2010, someone took the first step to sell their bitcoin. This would go down in history as the first time anyone would sell bitcoin. Laszlo Hanyecz sold 10,000 bitcoins juts for two pizzas. At its all-time-high exchange rate of $50,000 to 1 bitcoin, those tokens would have made Laszlo worth about $500 million. And in hindsight, you would agree that the decision was nothing but a hasty misstep.

Competitions Appeared On The Scene (2011)

As the popularity of Bitcoin grew and the notion of decentralized and encrypted currencies became more appealing, it was only a matter of time before other cryptocurrencies appeared as competitions.

Sometimes, these other cryptocurrencies are referred to as altcoins. They commonly attempt to expand on the initial Bitcoin structure. They do this by delivering terrific speed, anonymity, or other juicy benefits that paper money cannot offer. Among the first set of competitions that appeared were Litecoin and Namecoin. Presently, there are more than 1,000 cryptocurrencies in circulation, and new ones will keep coming into existence.

A Crash In Bitcoin Price (2013)

Right after the value of one Bitcoin touched the $1,000 landmark for the first time, the value soon started to fall. Many people who invested funds at this time incurred losses as the value dropped to around $300. It would take another two years before the value would reach $1000 again.

It was around this period that a new cryptocurrency slang will emerge: HODL. The first user of the term, apparently intoxicated, implied that he was holding his coins and not selling despite the price crash. The term is now popularly used to refer to keeping your cryptocurrency.

Case of Theft and Scams (2014)

As you already know, anonymity and minimal regulation are major features of cryptocurrency. So, there's a possibility that these features may encourage illicit crypto dealings. And that was exactly the case in the early days of 2014, the biggest Bitcoin exchange worldwide, Mt.Gox, went offline. After this, the holders of 850,000 units of Bitcoins lost all their coins.

Investigations are yet to get to the root of what went wrong exactly. But, regardless of what the true story was, someone had fraudulently gotten their hands on a large loot. At that time, the whole haul was priced at 450 million dollars. You can only imagine what the loot will be hurt in today's figures.

The Emergence of Ethereum and ICOs (2016)

2016 was a reality check for Bitcoin. A new blockchain platform by the name of Ethereum came remarkably close to taking it all away from Bitcoin. In a flash, confidence swelled around the Ethereum platform. This platform employs cryptocurrency known as Ether to promote both blockchain-based apps and smart contracts.

Ethereum's emergence was amplified by the rise of Initial Coin Offerings (ICOs). ICOs are fundraising platforms that allow investors to buy cryptocurrency from a start-up hoping for a boost in value. Since then, ICOs have been a major part of launching a new cryptocurrency. ICOs are also commonly called Airdrops in the crypto world. They mean essentially the same thing, only that with airdrops, coins are distributed for free.

Here's a bonus tip: Grab an airdrop if you get to come across any. It costs you nothing but can save you everything.

Bitcoin attains an All-time High of $50,000 and continues to grow (2021 and Onwards)

A steady rise in the ways Bitcoin could serve as an effective medium of payment provided the boost cryptocurrency needed. That way, it continued to grow in popularity, even when the value was not as high as earlier peaks. Slowly, as more people found ways to use Bitcoin and other crypto coins, there was an influx of funds into the ecosystem.

In this period, the market peak value of all crypto coins rose astronomically. In 2017, it rose from $11bn to as high as over $300bn. Banks like Deutsche Bank, Barclays, BNP Paribas, and Citi Bank declared that they are seeking ways to possibly work with Bitcoin and other crypto coins. Simultaneously, the technology upon which Bitcoin was developed – Blockchain – spurred an uprising in the financial technology industry (and beyond). This uprising is only just the beginning of more advancements to be seen soon.

Prospects

Let's face it, you might have received diverse opinions on what Bitcoin and cryptocurrency are all about and what they will be in the future. Some people are confused about how genuine this technology is and if it will stand the test of time. When you surf the internet, you will find different resources posing different stances. For some, this technology is the future of money. For others, it's merely a temporary puff that will fade away.

However, you will never find an expert in financial matters who refers to cryptocurrency as a sham. That's because they very much understand the happenings in the DeFi world. The conspiracy theories you've heard are mostly propagated by those who benefit most from centralized paper currencies. So, to them, cryptocurrencies are a threat to their stability. If you're still uncertain about where you stand on cryptocurrencies, here are a few facts for you to consider.

First, Bitcoin as an asset has witnessed 4,600,000% since it came into being in 2009. No other asset in the history of money has recorded a 1,000,000% increase or in a decade as Bitcoin did. And as a plus, altcoins have achieved jaw-dropping percentage increases in value over the years.

Besides, there's still a long way for bitcoin and several other altcoins to reach their market capitalization (total value of outstanding assets). With the increasing trust by banks and multinational agencies, no doubt dealing in cryptocurrency is dealing in the future of money.

Having established the validity of this technology and its application (cryptocurrencies), several questions come to the fore. "Will it fulfill the potentials many early adopters had seen in it? In addition, will it replace government-regulated, centralized currency with an allotted and decentralized option regulated by market forces?

As recent happenings have indicated, blockchain technology and cryptocurrencies are the next big thing. For example, several businesses, applications, industries, and betting casinos are now accepting payments using cryptocurrencies. The most popular examples are Tesla, PayPal, Microsoft, KFC, and Twitch.

Therefore, what the future holds is non-debatable. It is a promising market with outstanding prospects. The most profitable advice you can get is to invest early enough in the technology.

Safety Concerns – Storage And Security Of Blockchain Data

Truly, blockchain technology is changing how we go about our business. Now, consumers can cut out the middleman in various essential services. This, in turn, reduces costs and increases efficiency. In this direction, a lot can change, thanks to blockchain technology. It wields the potential to alleviate poverty globally.

Then a question comes up almost immediately: if people will be exchanging it for goods and services, is it secure? To be more explicit, can blockchain-based technologies offer confidence and privacy at the same time to guarantee records that are confidential and cannot be tampered with? Having traced the history of blockchain technology and cryptocurrencies, one truth has been revealed. There is the possibility of a breach, but it's quite minimal. Compared to robbery and money laundering that occurs with paper currency, crypto assets are generally safer and more reliable.

For a clear understanding of how secure your blockchain data is, you must first understand how blockchain technology works. What exactly makes up a blockchain?

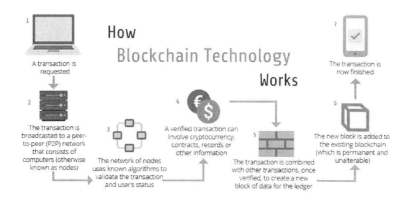

The best way to understand Blockchain is to see it as a decentralized ledger that can reduce costs by eliminating middlemen like banks. Blockchain literally puts the control of your assets directly in your control. The technology allows entries to the decentralized ledger. These entries are verified by the larger user-community instead of a central authority.

Every block stands for a transactional record, and the chain comes in as a link for all these transactional records. The decentralized computer network verifies the record and inputs the blocks of transactions in sequence. This is what results in the Blockchain. In the real sense of it, there is nothing of value on the Blockchain. The cryptocurrency bitcoin is merely an application of the blockchain technology

Now, is the block tamper-free? Honestly, it is not.

There is no such thing as perfect immutability. Just like it is with every other network, Blockchain is technically liable to mutation. But the fact that the computers, or nodes, on a blockchain network are widespread makes up for the security. The mathematical puzzle and computing ability needed to bring about these mutations make it practically impossible.

To cause changes to a chain, you would have to oversee over 51% of computers involved in a similarly widespread ledger. You again must make these changes to all the transactional records in a very brief period. For example, you have less than 10 minutes to alter the block for Bitcoin. To date, this breach has never been experienced, and to be sure, it's technically impossible.

In fact, you should understand that achieving both privacy and security of blockchain data simultaneously may be difficult in a traditional information network. Yet, Blockchain can do so by facilitating privacy through "public key infrastructure" that preserves against malicious tries to distort data. Again, by improving the size of a ledger, it becomes more distributed across the system, making it safer.

Common Market Terms To Know

A good understanding of the basics of blockchain technology and cryptocurrencies is incomplete if you do not know certain common market terms. Certain terminologies are exclusive to digital currency and do not have usage outside blockchain technology. These terms will keep appearing subsequently. Hence, you must understand what they mean to follow through.

Address

In cryptocurrency, an address is simply a wallet location where a user sends and collects cryptocurrency. Simply put, it is the crypto version of a cash bank account. These addresses are made up of a lengthy sequence of numbers and letters.

Altcoin

An altcoin is any other cryptocurrency that is not bitcoin. These include Ether and several other assets hosted on the Bitcoin and Ethereum chain networks. As it stands, there are over a thousand altcoins in place in the cryptocurrency world.

Arbitrage

In cryptocurrency, arbitrage is the term used to imply utilizing the opportunity of a price disparity between two distinct exchanges. For instance, assume bitcoin is selling for £7,650 on one exchange and £7,900 on another. A trader can perform arbitrage by buying the cryptocurrency on the first exchange, then, sell it on the second exchange. That way, this trader earns a fair profit.

ATH

"ATH" is an abbreviation that stands for the phrase "all-time high." This phrase can come in quite handy in tracking how the cryptocurrency market value rises and falls. These currencies are so volatile, so a good awareness of their ATH can be all you need to stay afloat.

A cryptocurrency could reach numerous local highs before hitting a new all-time high (ATH).

Blocks

Several cryptocurrencies employ the services of blocks. These blocks are made up of recorded digital transactions that have been verified.

Bear vs Bull

A bear market is experiencing a value recession or price decline. In crypto slang, this can be referred to as dips. Expert investors consider bearish markets as the best condition to purchase assets at a cheaper value in anticipation of when it snaps out of a recession. On the other hand, a bull market is on a steady rise and is economically viable.

Blockchain

Blockchain technology is basically a dispersed ledger network. It comprises a sequence of blocks. These blocks carry confirmed transactions. The Blockchain was constructed to be not only decentralized but also tamper-free. Therefore, entries cannot be removed once they have been recorded on this distributed ledger. The notion of blockchain technology came to the limelight in late 2008 when the bitcoin white paper was posted anonymously.

Cryptocurrency

A cryptocurrency is simply a currency that relies on cryptography for its creation. Bitcoin, for instance, utilizes the perks of cryptography to substantiate transactions.

Cryptography

Cryptography is essentially the technique of encoding and decoding data so that third parties cannot alter or read the data being transmitted.

Distributed Ledger

A distributed ledger is a network of recording data that is completely widespread or circulated across multiple distinct devices. The Blockchain is a good example of a distributed ledger.

Escrow

Escrow is a third-party that carries financial resources on behalf of the other two entities. In some cases, a third-party would have to carry funds in escrow, especially when there is a lack of trust between the other parties involved in the transaction.

Fiat Currencies

Fiat currencies are currencies with a set value. Fiat currencies are minted by a central bank. Fiat implies "by decree," and these currencies carry this value because some main authority has decided that they have a monetary value. Good examples of fiat currencies are the American Dollar, Euro, British Pounds, and the Japanese Yen.

Exchanges

Exchanges are practically the only marketplaces where crypto traders can make transactions involving cryptocurrencies. The largest cryptocurrency exchange globally is Binance, owned by one of the richest cryptocurrency investors in the world.

Gas Fees

A gas fee is a term peculiar to the Ethereum blockchain. It's a payment by crypto traders as compensation for the processing of transactions on the blockchain.

FOMO

The word "FOMO" is an abbreviation for the phrase "fear of missing out." This is a situation when investors begin to buy up a specific asset based on the prospects that it will increase in value. Getting caught up in the FOMO process can lead to very undesirable results. It's more desirable to study market conditions before deciding to invest.

Initial Coin Offering

An initial coin offering (ICO) depicts the first time an organization delivers crypto tokens to the public to raise funds.

Market Cap

Market cap is a contracted form that stands for market capitalization, a term for the total cumulative market value of a crypto asset.

Mining

Mining is the technique for developing new units of any cryptocurrency.

Mining Incentive

The mining incentive is that reward given to miners for verifying transactions and mining them into new blocks.

Moon/Mooning

When a cryptocurrency moons, it simply implies that there has been a sharp increase in its value.

Noob

Beginners in blockchain technology are often referred to as "noobs" by those that have stayed longer in the industry.

Pump and Dump

A "pump and dump" is a kind of investment strategy where one or more crypto trade or investors come together to boost the value of any crypto asset so they can sell it after its value has gone high artificially.

ROI

ROI is simply an abbreviation for "return on investment."

If you seek a means to tap into the potentials hidden in the world of cryptocurrency and blockchain technology, you must start from the basics. To get involved in cryptocurrency, you should be mindful of every single relevant industry terminology, as they can turn out to be helpful. However, your knowledge should not be limited to just the terminologies. You also should have enough understanding of cryptocurrency history and the security concerns that are present. These are the details you must be abreast of to thrive in this industry.

Chapter 2
How to Start Trading
Cryptocurrencies

"Well, I think it is working. There may be other currencies like it that may be even better. But in the meantime, there's a big industry around Bitcoin. — People have made fortunes off Bitcoin, some have lost money. It is volatile, but people make money off volatility too."
Richard Branson

Going by Richard Branson's assessment of cryptocurrencies (bitcoin in particular), there is certainly a lot for you to benefit from this chapter. And, if you have decided to get involved in trading cryptocurrencies, there are certain steps you must take to start your trading experience. The first step is to decide what cryptocurrency wallet will be the best for you. To do this, you must understand what a crypto wallet is, what it is used for, and what makes a crypto wallet standard and suitable for trading. Aside from this, you must then understand the concept of cryptocurrency exchanges and how to identify the best for you to trade your crypto coins.

In this chapter, I will expose you to the merits and pitfalls of various crypto wallet services. You would discover answers to the questions you have as you get set to start trading cryptocurrencies. It gets a lot easier from here!

Types of Cryptocurrency Wallets And How To Choose The Best For You

Cryptocurrencies like Bitcoin (BTC), Ethereum (ETH), Tether (USDT), Litecoin (LTC), etc., cannot be stored without a crypto wallet. And if you can't store crypto without a wallet, you definitely cannot trade either. There are various types of crypto wallets where you can collect and keep your crypto coins. However, it is more important to choose the best of these different types of crypto wallets to suit your trading needs and preferences.

To Start With, What Is a Crypto Wallet?

Crypto wallets are remarkably similar to how a vending machine works in a public place. Simply put, anyone can put in cash into the vending machine. Yet, you can only take-out money from the vending machine if you have the keys. This is how crypto wallets or digital wallets work.

Before you begin any trading or investment with any type of cryptocurrency, it is required that you get a space where you can store your crypto coins. That space, where you can lawfully confirm the presence of your cryptocurrencies and easily find out your crypto balance, is what is referred to as crypto or a digital wallet.

The Public And Private Keys

Digital wallets or crypto wallets contain two kinds of keys (private keys and public keys). These keys are what run the major activity that takes place in your crypto wallets. These special keys are used to receive cryptocurrencies and likewise send to other crypto wallets. They are similarly used to perform certain transactions on the blockchain system.

What then are these two special keys?

It is general knowledge that cryptocurrencies are not concrete items (they can't be touched). Likewise, all trades performed through these cryptocurrencies make up the digital ledgers you find on the blockchain system. So, a type of password is required to verify the presence of cryptocurrencies on the blockchain system. This is where private, and public keys come into play.

Every crypto wallet account comes with its unique address. This address is the crypto equivalent of the IBAN number used in physical banking processes. If you want someone to send you money, you do not need to share any other detail than your crypto wallet address.

Private and public keys are employed as passages to the deposits made into the crypto wallet account. They are again used to send money from the crypto wallet account to another account. It is impossible to perform any transaction without either of the private and the public key. Blockchain technology requires at least one of these two keys before any transaction can take place. Certain special encryption standards are used to link the public and private keys together. Due to this, you can access the public key information using the private key. But you cannot access the private key information using the public key.

In the cryptocurrency community, the private key is regarded as the most vital password. If, by any means, this private key is gotten by anyone aside from the crypto wallet account holder, all cryptocurrency deposits may be forfeited. And it is always impossible to get these deposits back. Thus, you must keep the private key safe and confidential. You must further ensure that no other person aside from you accesses this key.

In all, a cryptocurrency wallet is a software program, a hardware gadget, or an online platform where the two special keys used in sending and receiving different blockchain cryptocurrency tokens are stored.

Types of Cryptocurrency Wallets

There are several kinds of cryptocurrency wallets. This segment will explain the various crypto wallet technologies available and the pros and cons of using them.

Hardware Wallets

Hardware wallets are one of the most secure ways to keep cryptocurrencies. They are also referred to as "cold wallets". They are used offline, making them a safer storage facility than "hot wallets" (which includes web wallets and software wallets).

Pros

- They deliver increased in-built protection as you cannot access them without the correct password.

- They have excellent storage facilities.

Cons

- It is an expensive type of cryptocurrency wallet. Yet, it tends to offer real value for your money.

- When they get corrupted, it might be impossible to retrieve all that is in them. The same happens if you forget your passcode. If you think it can't get any worse, there's the story of Stefan Thoman. He forgot the password to his bitcoin wallets worth over $220 million.

- As physical storage devices, chances are that you might misplace them.

Recommended Hardware Wallets

- Ledger Nano S

- Trezor wallet

- KeepKey

Software Wallets

Software crypto wallets are also known as "hot wallets". This is because they are used through the internet. This remote use makes them victims of hacks and cyber-attacks. However, if you plan to trade in low quantities, desktop software crypto wallets would be perfect for you!

My number one recommended software wallet would be Coinbase. This is due to the numerous perks it provides to you as a crypto trader. Other recommended software wallets include:

- Electrum (not for beginners due to its technicalities)

- Exodus

Mobile Phone Wallets or App-based Wallets

Mobile phone wallets or app-based wallets are the most popular types of crypto wallets. And from their name, they are used on phones as applications.

Binance is a first-choice mobile phone wallet for most cryptocurrency investors. And the reasons are undeniable. Binance hosts the largest cryptocurrency exchange in the world, as you must now know. It also runs its own Smart Chain and incredibly low transfer fees, unlike other blockchains. Others include Jaxx Liberty, Mycelium, Copay, and Cryptonator.

Web Wallets

Web wallets are not completely safe. Here, the reality is that you never get access to your personal private keys. We recommend them only as a temporary space to move cryptocurrencies from one place to another. Regardless, it still all boils down to how well you trust whichever provider you choose.

With hacking incidences that befell Mt. Gox and Coincheck in 2020, Coinbase is the only provider I can recommend in this category.

Paper Wallets

Paper wallets will easily pass as one of the most secure ways of keeping your cryptocurrency safe. They are used offline to hold cryptocurrencies. Simply put, it is precisely the printing of QR codes that stand for your private and public keys. This offline safety system implies that you have complete custody of your cryptocurrencies. Paper wallets are one of the best cryptocurrency wallet setups out there!

However, you should note that a paper wallet will not be the best option for every crypto trader. If you plan to trade every day or every week, paper wallets are not the best for you. This crypto wallet setup is most suitable for those who want to be long-term cryptocurrency investors. Another point to note is that you must be extremely careful when using this kind of wallet. Any damage, either through water, fire, or any other kind, can lead to you losing all your digital assets and investments.

In all, hot wallets (desktop software wallets and app/web-based wallets) are not completely secure crypto wallet options. They are only suitable for small-scale trades. Cold wallets (hardware wallets and paper wallets), on the other hand, are safer options and will work well for long-term investors. It is left to you to decide which wallet works best for your type of investment.

Cryptocurrency Exchanges

Cryptocurrency exchanges are online platforms where you can buy, sell, and trade your cryptocurrencies. It is imperative to note that crypto exchanges are not built similarly. Therefore, certain factors must be considered in deciding whether a cryptocurrency exchange can satisfy your unique set of needs as a crypto trader. These factors to be considered include:

- The type

- The features

- The security regulations in place.

Types of Exchanges

Brokerage

Some exchanges permit traders to buy or sell straight from the platform. This gives room for one-time trades and is most suitable if you are just beginning to trade. Investors are usually required to verify their investment accounts by submitting personal identification details.

Peer to Peer

Commonly referred to as P2P, these platforms work perfectly for those who are primarily concerned with their privacy. Peer to Peer exchanges permits one-on-one trading relationships where two traders select a particular price and mode for payment independently.

Some P2P exchanges are classified according to location. That way, you get to meet other crypto traders at a particular geographical point. Most P2P platforms proceed slightly by fostering the trade and functioning as an escrow and mediator when there is a disagreement. Your privacy is generally guaranteed on these platforms. Still, the burden of your security and that of your cryptocurrencies is on your shoulder.

Full Trading Platform

Full trading platforms create an environment featuring many traders coming together to trade among themselves on the platform, just as it is in an actual stock market. Full trading exchanges employ an order book to correspondingly buy and sell orders. The bigger full trading platforms even deliver several features such a margin trading, special order types, customizable graphs, etc. As a beginner trader, you will not need most of these features.

Nuggets To Note While Choosing A Cryptocurrency Exchange

Features

Platforms offering many features (margin trading, complex charts, and advanced order types) are advisable for very professional traders. This is as you will need to have a deep knowledge of how the crypto industry works to utilize these features. For beginner traders, the lesser the features of the exchange, the better.

Functionality

Whether you are a beginner or a professional, you need to first confirm if a platform can function for the transaction you want to perform before you choose it. Most importantly, you may want to consider if the exchange accepts your currency.

Fees

Every platform has a unique fee structure meant for different types of traders on their platform. You must check what the fee structure is on a cryptocurrency exchange platform before choosing it.

Privacy

It is indeed practically impossible for you to keep trading without anyone knowing who you are. Yet, you need to ensure that there is a good level of privacy offered before you choose any cryptocurrency exchange.

Security

A side-effect of anonymity in the crypto world is that security is always vital when trading cryptocurrencies. You should assess all the same factors when selecting an exchange as you do with a crypto wallet. However, there is one significant difference. Exchange is designed for quick and simple transactions, which imply that occasionally security may be compromised.

Key Storage

A standard exchange will combine all user assets from the whole platform. Then, withdraw a large percentage and keep it in a cold wallet. That way, if the platform is attacked, the loss is minimal, if any.

Insurance

Truly, cryptocurrencies are still very recent. Hence, a large part of the industry is unregulated. So, to a large extent, the responsibility of your insurance is in your own hands. Yet, some exchanges that adhere to government regulations provide insurance services for your funds. And a few others have 3rd party insurance packages for your crypto assets.

User Experience

This factor is divided into three parts. First, as a beginner, you want to be certain that you are using an exchange with a basic layout and user interface. That way, you can successfully navigate through the exchange platform. An experienced trader will enjoy an advanced and sophisticated interface. Secondly, you should check what others have to say about the crypto exchange services. Check out their ratings to know if they will serve you well. Finally, check out their customer service. How do they handle disputes? Are they always readily available?

Chapter 3
The Importance of Trading Strategies

"The game of speculation is the most uniformly fascinating game in the world. But it is not a game for the stupid, the mentally lazy, the person of inferior emotional balance, or the get-rich-quick adventurer. They will die poor."

Jesse Livermore

Jesse Livermore is passing one important message here – self-discipline, meticulousness, and strategizing are vital aspects of any trading activity. These three concepts are interrelated in the way they operate. Only a disciplined trader will pay keen attention to every detail. By paying keen attention to every detail, you can develop a strategy that guides how you trade your digital assets moving forward.

There are numerous means to invest in cryptocurrency and achieve maximum return on your investments. Trading strategies enable you to coordinate those processes into a coherent blueprint that you can follow. By being religious with your coherent blueprint, you can properly control and get the best out of your cryptocurrency strategy. Since there are numerous distinct trading strategies, I will take you through all you need to know about the most common strategies for trading cryptocurrency. Nevertheless, some of these strategies may likewise work with other financial assets, like options, stock, forex, or precious metals like diamond and gold.

In this chapter, you will gain insight into the rudiments of trading and all you need to win at this game of speculation (the crypto markets). With a sensible trading strategy, you've got a greater chance at achieving maximum return on your investments in the crypto market.

What Is A Trading Strategy and Its Importance?

A trading strategy is a comprehensive plan that guides every part of your trading activities. It is a blueprint you develop to lead you through all your trading investments.

A major benefit of a trading strategy is that it helps mitigate financial risk. A trading strategy simply gets rid of a ton of needless decisions. While having a trading strategy is not a required criterion for trading, it can be a lifesaver more than you can imagine. If something accidental occurs in the market (which will occur), your trading strategy should specify how you respond to such a situation. Your emotions should not direct how you react.

In other words, a trading strategy in place gets you ready for the likely developments. It discourages you from making irrational, emotional decisions that mostly result in huge financial losses.

For examplo, a thorough trading strategy should answer the following questions:

1. What kinds of assets should you trade?

2. What structure do you take?

3. What mechanisms and pointers do you utilize?

4. What prompts your entries and exits?

5. What decides your position sizing?

6. How do you record and estimate your portfolio performance?

While there are distinctions between crypto trading and investment strategies, crypto trading basically refers to buying and selling crypto assets to achieve amazing returns. These returns, on the other hand, are exactly the results that trading strategies bring to fruition.

Types of Trading Strategies

There are two types of trading strategies I will be exposing you to in this book.

- The Active Trading Strategies

- The Passive Trading Strategies

If you consider the explanations I gave earlier concerning trading strategies, one thing is clear. Trading strategies aren't a rigid procedure. In fact, you can create a merger between these trading strategies. What might work for you may be a cross strategy where you combine different strategies.

Active Trading Strategies

Active trading strategies need additional time and awareness. I call them active as they require steady scrutiny and regular portfolio supervision.

Day Trading

Day trading is by far the most popular active trading strategy. It is a widespread error to believe that all active traders are simply day traders. This is not true in any way. Day trading involves entering positions and exiting on the same day. Due to this, day traders try to make the most of intraday price movements (every time the price moves within a single trading day).

The phrase "day trading" comes from the everyday markets, where trading is only allowed within certain hours of the day. In these traditional markets, day traders do not trade overnight when trading is stopped. This situation is slightly different from the cryptocurrency trading markets. Trading in the crypto markets runs through the entire 24 hours of each day and for the entire 365 days in a year. Hence, when we say day trading in the crypto markets, we refer to it in a slightly different context. It is generally a short-term trading style, where crypto traders enter and exit positions within a timeframe of 24 hours or less.

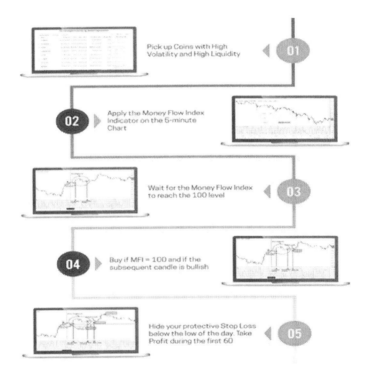

As a day trader, you generally utilize price movement and technical analysis in creating your trade indications. Besides, you may use several other methods to uncover inefficiencies in the market. The day trading strategy for trading cryptocurrency can be very productive for some.

Still, it's a rather tiring, demanding process that involves taking high risks. As such, day trading is only advisable for more experienced crypto traders.

Swing Trading

Swing trading is a type of trading strategy that lasts for a longer period. Here, traders hold positions for more than a day but generally not more than a couple of weeks or one month. In certain ways, swing trading is a balance between day trading and trend trading.

Swing trading is likely the most practical and simple active trading strategy for beginners. Since swing trades take a longer time to play out, traders have enough time to review their decisions. In most cases, traders have sufficient time to respond to how the trade is progressing. With swing trading, traders can make decisions with less urgency and extra thoughtfulness

Trend Trading

Sometimes also called position trading, trend trading is a strategy that sees traders hold positions for an extended period, commonly a few months at least. As the name would indicate, trend traders strive to make the most of directional trends. Trend traders may assume a long position in an uptrend and then take a short position in a downtrend. Trend trading can be the best for beginner traders if they appropriately do their homework and mitigate risk.

Scalping

Scalping is one of the hastiest trading strategies you can find around. Scalpers don't aim to make use of huge moves or drawn-out trends. Instead, this strategy concentrates on capitalizing on small movements repeatedly. For instance, making profits off gaps in liquidity, bid-ask spreads, or other inefficiencies in the crypto market. Scalping is a developed trading strategy that isn't suitable for beginner traders due to its intricacies. It again employs a serious knowledge of the workings of the crypto markets.

Passive Trading Strategies

Passive trading strategies encourage a further hands-off procedure. By this, portfolio management takes up a shorter timeframe and less awareness.

Buy and hold

"Buy and hold" is a passive trading strategy where crypto traders buy a crypto asset with the plan to hold it for a long period, not minding market fluctuations. This strategy is commonly employed in long-term trading and investment portfolios. There, the motive is solely to get in the market without paying any attention to the timing. This strategy's notion is that the timing or entry value will not make much difference in a long enough time.

Index investing

Generally, index investing implies buying ETFs and indices in the regular markets. However, this type of property is also accessible in the cryptocurrency markets. It is accessible both on centralized cryptocurrency exchanges and the Decentralized Finance (DeFi) movement.

As a crypto investor or trader, you can use crypto indexes by investing in a privacy coin index rather than selecting a particular privacy coin. This way, you can stake on privacy coins as a sector while ridding yourself of the risk of staking on just one coin.

Formulating a crypto trading strategy that works to achieve your financial goals and suits your style is not a simple task. I have gone through some of the most popular crypto trading strategies. Hopefully, you can pick out which of them may work best for you. To discover which strategy works and which doesn't, you should observe and follow every trading strategy, ensuring that you keep all the rules you set.

Finally, it's worthy of note that you are not mandated to stick to the same strategies forever. You should be prepared to revise and modify your strategies. In other words, your trading strategies should always advance as you gain further trading experience.

Chapter 4

Understanding Cryptocurrency Market Trends

"The market is new, meaning that its highs and lows are very pronounced. A far smaller marketplace, cryptocurrency exchanges are also vulnerable to the trade movements of 'whale' traders. This means that the whole market can be vulnerable to the trade decisions of those heavily invested."

Cointree

The above statement by Cointree perfectly illustrates the whole twists and turns involved in the crypto market. As Cointree has viewed it, the crypto market is a new one. Hence, every high and every low (trends) make an obvious difference affecting how the market progresses. This factor, there is the part where a single move by a major investor to either buy or sell could trigger a major rise (pump) or a major fall (dip) in the value of whatever cryptocurrency is involved. In all, these all go on to depict how important market trends can be in the world of cryptocurrency. Therefore, a good crypto trader must understand these different market trends and know how to utilize them for the best possible outcome.

In several ways, the crypto market is not different from the regular stock market. Yes, the essential assets traded in both markets are different, however, the analysis employed to track the value of different assets is pretty much a similar process. If you employ these similar principles, you are sure to get the best possible outcomes.

The Crypto Market vs The Stock Market

Trading is one process that has remained relevant in centuries of the economic process, maybe even since everything began to exist. The concept of stock exchange is somewhat recent, and even more recent is the concept of cryptocurrency exchange. (They're still quite in their early stage.) And even though they have various things in common, there are yet certain distinctions. Understanding where these two are related and where they are different will enable you to make intelligent discoveries while analyzing.

The essential asset is the major point of distinction between crypto and stock exchanges. While stock exchanges trade shares of organizations, cryptocurrency exchanges trade currency. Possibly the greatest point of variance (till now) is the notion of unpredictability. Even though, stock exchanges can persist on long bull or bear markets, they commonly happen in gradual processes. On the other hand, crypto exchanges can undergo prominent changes in a very short time.

On the bright side, with time, there are increasingly substantial data ready for analysis. With increased data, it becomes likely to generate more refined algorithms for trading and predictive signals to neutralize some of the markets' volatility.

How to Investigate, Research, And Analyze Data For The Best Possible Outcome

Investing and trading cryptocurrencies remain recognized as very unpredictable and uncertain. But while every individual crypto coin deals with the threat of decline, virtually all experts on the matter accept that cryptocurrency is the path that leads to the future. It's not a question of whether cryptocurrencies will be a staple asset over a decade from now. It's merely a question of what coins will be more prominent and when this will come to play.

As you investigate, research, and analyze crypto, consider the crypto markets like you would stock exchanges, and contemplate involving certain techniques for your analysis. There are three major methods of analyzing data for the best possible outcome. Thankfully, they aren't overly complex terms.

Technical Analysis

Under technical analysis, you're researching the trends and patterns in the stats, as well as investigating historical quantity and actions, including how the value moves and swings. You do these to make informed projections on the direction the value is going in the short run and in the long run. You will need to decide which specialized trading methods suit your trading skillset. Fibonacci retracement trading is one to try.

According to RJO Futures, "Fibonacci retracement trading is a popular technical tool used by traders to determine price action. Fibonacci retracement trading is taking two extreme points from a contract's price, usually a high and a low, then dividing it by a Fibonacci ratio to determine support and resistance levels."

The strategy of analyzing instabilities in value is a perfect fit for crypto. Yet, you must be swift in making your move. Considering the high unpredictability, assistance and resistance levels can encounter huge highs and lows.

Fundamental Analysis

When using fundamental analysis, you are not watching for the direction of the value of crypto assets, per se. Rather, you're aiming to realize what's aiding this valuation. To put another way, what structures are the financials playing tricks in the background? Thanks to this analysis, you can specify if the data indicates that the crypto is undervalued or overvalued in that period.

Sentimental Analysis

In this method, even though you need to be meticulous with sentimental analysis while investing in stocks, it can surely be a rather beneficial tool in the exchange of cryptocurrency. In this analysis, you are observing more than just the numbers. Now you want to observe major players speculate and believe. These players may include investors, economists, journalists, hedge fund managers, and influencers.

To sum it up, you can't speculate that cryptocurrency exchange will run just like it happens in the exchange of stocks. Volatility is way increased and, while the upside is quite larger, the negative side is very sudden. Having said this, by using any of these analysis techniques in your trading activity, you increase chances of success.

Common Trading Mistakes And How to Avoid Them

"Crypto market does not forgive even an honest mistake."
Anonymous

The idea behind this quote has unsettled a ton of beginner traders. Most of them might have taken an early bow due to the fear of making any mistake at all. For others, they have failed to stay vigilant, leading them to losses that have forced them to take an early bow too. My advice is for you to keep this mantra in mind. It helps you avoid many needless mistakes you would have made, either unwittingly or otherwise. Again, I will expose you to some of these crypto trading mistakes; you should avoid making the same blunders as losing crypto traders.

Before I go deeper into this subject, there is one additional thing you must be mindful of. And that is the fact that you should avoid making a lot of mistakes in a short timeframe (also known as unaware trading). This might affect you so bad that you will be unable to get back to crypto trading again. A lot has been earned through crypto trading and investing, and if you care to look, a lot has also been lost.

Mostly, those who view this as a mathematical and mindset concept make wealth, while those who offer an impracticable perspective to trading end up sacrificing their hard-earned funds. Many rich folks in the world are hedge fund managers (traders), and they achieved this feat by sticking to their trading strategies and reducing their losses to the barest minimum. The simplest way to lessen your losses is by understanding crypto trading as a system and drawing lessons from your mistakes and others. Note, the latter is preferable.

Have this in mind, *"Learning from your mistakes is smartness, and learning from other mistakes is wisdom."*

Crypto Trading Mistakes to Avoid

Beginning With Actual Cash Before Paper Trading

Trading is a technique, just like any other technique; it requires unlimited hours of training and patience to gain full mastery of it. There are also ground rules, and one of them is using paper trading first before using actual cash. This aspect is tiring for many beginner traders, but it is probably the most decisive part of crypto trading. A lot of beginner traders who don't mind losing their funds end up going into trades with their real money before sharpening their skills and mastery. This is wrong!

Failure to Utilize Stop Loss In Risk Management

If you are yet to find out, the holy grail of risk-management in crypto trading are stop losses. Stop-loss assists you in minimizing your loss when your forecasted trade falls through. This is not about how convinced you are about trade being successful. Failing to use a stop loss is the biggest mistake you can ever make as a crypto trader.

Spending Too Much On Brokerage Fees

Brokerage fees when they are too much can take out a considerable amount of your trading income. The solution here is to employ broker (exchange) services that provide a low trading fee and maintain a high volume and liquidity. By doing this, you will end up earning more profits from your trades. Here are some exchanges that provide the lowest brokerage fees around:

- Binance = 0.1%

- CEX = 0.25%

Failure to View Profit/Loss as a Percentage:

Here is another typical blunder beginner that traders make. They always view their profit and loss, as a total gain, instead of viewing it as a percentage profit or loss. Cultivate the habit of viewing every trade as a percentage growth, and you will have a detailed view of your profit and losses.

Failure to Perform Fundamental Analysis

Several beginner traders begin by selecting a well-known cryptocurrency and begin to trade them. There is the likelihood that for a long time, you will end up earning good money. But keep in mind that a sharp, devastating decline may bring the price way below ground Zero. The way to prevent this noobie crypto trading mistake is by performing fundamental analysis of the coin you are about to start trading.

Find out:

- What does this coin do?

- The prospective expectation of the Cryptocurrency

- The team managing it

- Token economy

When you follow these parameters, you can now make a list of tokens that you would prefer to trade. Always keep this in mind. Trading is not the same for everyone. So, you must design your own system.

Trading Using Pump and Dump Signals

Telegram is the go-to communication medium for cryptocurrency traders globally. There are certain Telegram groups around you that give signals for buying and selling crypto. The main question is: Do they work? And the answer is a big NO! Especially for a beginner trader, it is better if you can avoid such pump and dump programs. These groups are not realistic. When several users are trading based on one exact trading call, the possibilities of those "Signals" working is close to zero.

- Failing To Keep A Trading Journal

This is probably the biggest blunder most beginner crypto traders make. Jotting down the reason you are taking a trade and evaluating them later, enables you to find out:

- Why are certain trades delivering outstanding outcomes?

- Why are you losing on certain trades?

Keeping a trading journal will enable you to expand your trading strategy as time goes on. You can make use of a spreadsheet or just use a paper journal. This technique has proven to advance a beginner to the next stage of crypto trading proficiency.

Chapter 5

What You need to know about ICOs, STOs and IEOs

"There is a silent battle between three tokenized fundraising methods. How well you can benefit from these tokens as an investor can be the huge difference you need financially."

Anonymous

One part of this revelation you might not have noticed is the importance of knowing enough first. First, you must inquire into the contrast between these three tokenized fundraising strategies. Then, you seek ways to benefit from their rising fame as a crypto investor or trader. Following these steps is your perfect blueprint for making the best use of these three tokenized fundraising offerings.

Undoubtedly, the rise of Blockchain technology has shifted the paradigm in the business realm. The growth of technology and the rise in Blockchain fame has provided businesses with new means of raising funds. Now they can raise funds from both the public and a combination of high-profile traders and investors. The increasing prominence of Blockchain technology has brought us closer to the reality of concepts like ICOs, STOs, and IEOs. So, what are these fundraising methods, and how applicable are they to the present economic state? Are they different in any way from one another? If yes, then in what ways and more importantly, which method is the best?

Initial Coin Offerings (ICOs)

The evolution of ICOs dates to 2014 as an innovative fundraising method. ICOs create a different method from what used to be (Venture Capital and the Initial Public Offering). The ICOs soon became successful late into 2017 and in the early days of 2018. The ICO method attained a massive feat when it came to fundraising by giving rise to the benefit of fewer upfront capital requirements and an almost insignificant regulatory provision. During the boom, ICO programs have garnered over a massive $25 billion and boosted the gross crypto market cap to more than $800 billion.

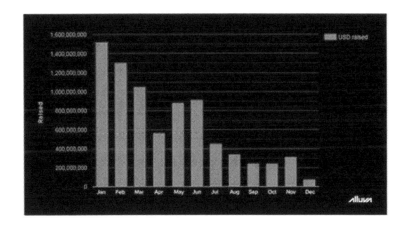

But the fortune of ICOs was short-lived. By the close of 2018, the world saw the collapse of ICOs. The collapse was caused by several ICO exit cons, legal obscurity, dishonest token deals and malicious pursuit of many ICO organizers defrauding their investors, resulting in investors instantly losing interest in ICOs. Aside from this, there were various backlashes and regulatory obstacles faced by ICOs in nations like the US, China, and South Korea.

Security Token Offerings (STOs)

Security Token Offerings (STOs) came as a substitute for the collapsing ICO model in 2018. STOs also came due to the discovery that regulatory adherence is unavoidable in the financial world. STOs drifted attention in the first four months of 2018. Eventually, they attained the height of popularity in November 2018. In an STO, investors receive security tokens different from the utility token given by ICOs. The security tokens are the crypto tokens reserved in a blockchain. It is then stimulated by some essential assets that carry some monetary price in the actual world.

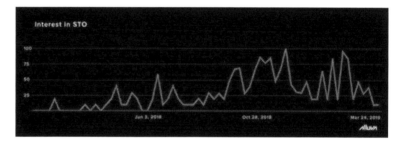

The STOs were able to offer investors improved safety and a considerable degree of clarity in the entire Tokenized fundraising market. The STOs are registered and endorsed by the Swiss Financial Market Supervisory Authority (FINMA) and the United States Securities and Exchange Commission (SEC). These STOs must operate in agreement with the regulatory protocols as demanded by the FINMA and SEC.

The extra benefit of protection and clarity for the investors with STOs comes with the increased cost and legal complicatedness. The regulatory compliances also restrict the partakers in an STO to just institutional investors. You should also note that security tokens can only be recorded on regulated cryptocurrency exchanges. This is as they can then adequately confirm the accreditation of the investor.

Initial Exchange Offerings (IEOs)

Initial Exchange Offerings are the most modern invention in the tokenized fundraising market inextricably associated with a particular exchange. In an IEO, a project's token sale is performed instantly on an exchange platform. The exchange requires those issuing the token to pay a listing surcharge together with a fraction of the tokens sold during the IEO. In place of the surcharge, the projects are traded on the exchange's platforms instantly, and the coins are recorded instantly after the IEO is completed. Whereas in an ICO, the tokens are recorded on exchanges many months after the ICO is completed.

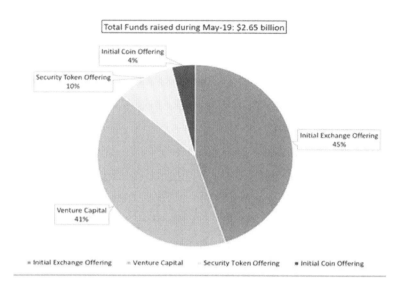

Total Funds raised during May-19: $2.65 billion

Initial Coin Offering 4%

Security Token Offering 10%

Initial Exchange Offering 45%

Venture Capital 41%

▪ Initial Exchange Offering   ▪ Venture Capital   Security Token Offering   ▪ Initial Coin Offering

IEOs don't make use of smart contracts to share tokens after the token sale. Instead, IEO partakers are given access to their balances. All they have to do is to log into their exchange account wallet. For investors to participate in an IEO and enjoy a streamlined experience, they need to finish the KYC (Know Your Customer) verifications and other inspections at the exchange stage.

ICOs, STOs and IEOs: Which Is The Best For You As A Crypto Investor

The increasing interest of investors indicates that both STOs and IEOs are better fundraising models for a project. ICOs have discovered and boosted the growth of the crypto economy. But, IEOs and STOs are economic forces to reckon with. As used by prominent and blooming ICOs such as NXT, ARK, Ethereum, etc., the tokenized fundraising models transformed the tokenized market. The ICOs provide investors of every sort, with cryptocurrency in their wallet, autonomy to take part in the token sale.

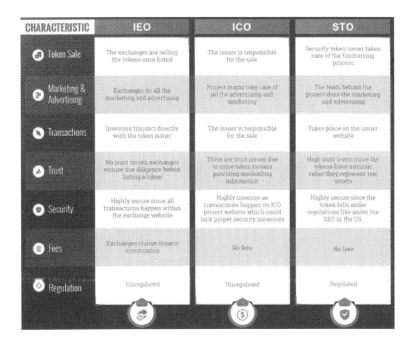

CHARACTERISTIC	IEO	ICO	STO
Token Sale	The exchanges are selling the tokens once listed	The issuer is responsible for the sale	Security token issuer takes care of the fundraising process
Marketing & Advertising	Exchanges do all the marketing and advertising	Project teams take care of all the advertising and marketing	The team behind the project does the marketing and advertising
Transactions	Investors transact directly with the token issuer	The issuer is responsible for the sale	Takes place on the issuer website
Trust	No trust issues, exchanges ensure due diligence before listing a token	There are trust issues due to some token issuers providing misleading information	High trust levels since the tokens have intrinsic value/they represent real assets
Security	Highly secure since all transactions happen within the exchange website	Highly insecure as transactions happen on ICO project website which could lack proper security measures	Highly secure since the token falls under regulations like under the SEC in the US.
Fees	Exchanges charge issuers commission	No fees	No fees
Regulation	Unregulated	Unregulated	Regulated

Even as STOs are not so prominent due to its relatively complicated and expensive execution compared with IEOs and ICOs, it still operates within a regulated frame. The security tokens provided by STOs carry real value as they are supported by a company's investments. The STOs are the most reliable as it operates within the legal framework of the FINMA and SEC.

However, the trend of IEOs is fast-rising, as its execution is simpler than STOs and more secure than ICOs. Anyone with a verified account with a cryptocurrency exchange and an amount of cryptocurrency in their wallet can participate in an IEO. The other merit provided by IEOs, unlike ICOs, is that the tokens are recorded as soon as a token sale is complete and can be used for trading. The drawback faced by IEO is that the tokens are not covered by some substantial value, like STOs.

The tokenized market is a new terrain for many investors. And all three models (ICOs, STOs, and IEOs) provide companies with a simple way of raising funds for their projects. All three have their own merits. The ICOs are free of bureaucracy and are not regulated, allowing ordinary people into the fundraising scheme. But the absence of regulation has resulted in numerous Ponzi schemes and fraudulent projects.

Comparison between ICO, IEO and STO

	ICO (Initial Coin Offering)	IEO (Initial Exchange Offering)	STO (Security Token Offering)
Definition	Crowdfunding by issuing utility token/coin	Crowdfunding by issuing utility token/coin via cryptocurrency exchange	Crowdfunding via issuing asset-backed token/coin
Difficulty to Set Up	Easy	Medium	Hard
Fundraising Cost	Low	Medium	High
Investor Protection	Low	Medium	High
Investor Accessibility	High	Medium	Low
Regulation Level	Low	Medium	High
Governance Level	Loose	Medium	Tight
Liquidity	Medium	High	Low

STOs settle the biggest difficulty of the lack of any assurances and repayment if a project falls through or turns out to be a scam. Yet, it turns out to be expensive as regards execution. IEO is seeing a quick surge in fame. It is a refined form of token offering where an exchange handles the token sale independently. The future of the tokenized economy is developing with various projects appearing with new inklings to launch a profitable fundraising procedure. It would be fascinating to see how the tokenized economy scenario grows in the coming years! What will be more fascinating is how well you can tap into the potential as a crypto investor.

The Legality Of ICOs Across The Globe

Having understood how all three tokenized models operate, we now shift our attention to ICOs. How are ICOs treated legally in different parts of the world?

Initial Coin Offerings (ICOs) have been very prominent over the last few years before new models were introduced. Over this period, ICOs have generated approximately US$4 billion worldwide. A rising number of start-ups in the blockchain realm and beyond are going for the novel fundraising tool rather than the initial venture capital strategy.

But as ICOs increase in fame, these are coming to be a major sector of focus for regulators around the world who are cautioning that the practice is unregulated in many jurisdictions. Regulation is arriving very quickly for cryptocurrencies and ICOs, and countries have adopted various strategies.

What then are the legalities of ICOs and cryptocurrencies in different parts of the world?

China

The People's Bank of China prohibited all ICO transactions in 2017 and instructed that cryptocurrency exchanges be closed. However, in 2018, China formulated a set of legislations to take effect that year. That legislation should lift the embargo on ICOs.

South Korea

Following the path China took, South Korea's Financial Services Commission declared in September 2017 the ban of ICOs, but reports, later on, saw the ban get eased months later.

European Union

In the EU, ICOs are permitted if they comply with AML/KYC policies.

Switzerland

The Swiss Financial Market Supervisory Authority (FINMA) published ICO policies in 2018. These policies detail how the authority is overseeing ICOs and cryptocurrencies based on their purpose and transferability.

Liechtenstein

ICOs are legal in Lichtenstein, but banking on the rights linked to a certain token, relevance of securities and financial instrument law may stand involved.

Germany

ICOs are permitted in Germany. Regulation related to a token is conditional on the rights the cryptocurrency carries. An ICO may be required to conform to existing regulations such as the Investment Act, Securities Trading Act, Prospectus Act, Payment Services Supervision Act, and Banking Acts.

Estonia

ICOs are permitted in Estonia, and the government is even contemplating performing its own token sale to generate funds.

Lithuania

ICOs are permitted in Lithuania. In certain cases, existing laws restricting securities and money laundering may be relevant.

Russia

ICOs are legal in Russia, but the government is structuring a regulatory system.

United Kingdom

ICOs are legal in the United Kingdom. The UK Financial Conduct Authority has handed out a warning to crypto investors, asserting that ICO projects are still observed and could be risky to investors.

Gibraltar

ICOs are permitted in Gibraltar. In October 2017, the government created a framework for governing distributed ledger technology firms, which came into effect in 2018.

Isle of Man

ICOs are legal in the Isle of Man. The country has plans to develop a framework to regulate this sector.

United States of America

ICOs are legal in the United States, but legislations differ completely from state to state. On the federal tier,

ICOs are required to be registered and authorized first. This comprises enlisting with the Securities and Exchange Commission if the ICO must sell or trade securities. ICO organizers are also directed to comply with AML/KYC procedures.

Canada

ICOs are legal in Canada. The Canadian Securities Administration refers to a four-factor test in deciding if a cryptocurrency has to be enlisted as securities.

Abu Dhabi

The Financial Services Regulatory Authority (FSRA) of the Emirate of Abu-Dhabi hopes to create regulations for cryptocurrencies and ICOs. According to the Abu Dhabi regulator, cryptocurrencies are "commodities", and major parts of ICOs will be organized as "specified investments."

Israel

ICOs are legal in Israel, but the government seeks to have regulations in place. The Israeli Securities Authority has declared that a panel was established to investigate how ICOs function in the country.

Singapore

ICOs are permitted in Singapore. In 2017, the Monetary Authority of Singapore (MAS) published protocols scrutinizing cryptocurrencies and ICOs. The protocols direct that cryptocurrencies that are "capital market products" under the Securities and Futures Act can be controlled under the MAS.

Japan

In 2017, the Financial Services Authority said that relying on the structure employed, ICOs may be governed under Japanese law, also by the Financial Instruments and Exchange Act and the Payment Services Act. The authority is likewise contemplating ICO restrictions. Japan adopted cryptocurrency regulations in 2017, accepting it as a legal payment method. The law compels cryptocurrency exchanges to carry a special license to function.

Thailand

ICOs are permitted in Thailand, but they are not regulated. The central bank is planning a structure to enforce regulations on cryptocurrencies.

Philippines

ICOs are legal in the Philippines, but authorities have said that certain tokens might be examined as securities and must adhere to securities registration guidelines.

Hong Kong

ICOs are permitted in Hong Kong. Authorities have announced that some tokens might be securities and must be regarded as such.

Australia

ICOs are legal in Australia, but if an ICO or cryptocurrency is categorized under the Corporations Act, further disclosures are activated. For example, an ICO might prompt a disclosure provision if the ICO falls in a Managed Investment Scheme MIS category.

Chapter 6

Risk Management in Cryptocurrency Trading

"You never know what kind of setup market will present to you; your objective should be to find an opportunity where risk-reward ratio is best."

Jaymin Shah

When an experienced crypto trader speaks, one factor is always obvious. Undoubtedly, that factor is the certainty with which they deliver advice. Jaymin Shah, as an experienced trader, has assessed how volatile the crypto market terrain can be. Hence, he has accepted the huge relevance of an excellent risk management strategy in cryptocurrency trading. An excellent risk management strategy is particularly important for every crypto trader or investor who seeks to achieve maximum return on their investments. The rules surrounding the risks involved in cryptocurrency trading don't have to be difficult to adhere to. This chapter will examine the risks associated with trading and how you can handle your cryptocurrency assets to achieve wonderful returns.

To start with, what is risk in trading? Risk in trading is simply the likelihood of an unfavorable incidence occurring in your trading activities. It is the chance that an event might go against your plans or speculations. Risk is an inevitable part of the world of crypto and its markets. In crypto trading, the risk is the possibility of an adverse result on your trade or investment, which results in losses. For example, a 50% risk on a short position means a 50% chance that the price of Bitcoin will rise, leading to a loss on your own end.

This chapter will teach you about basic principles that guide risk management while trading Crypto

Types of Risk

The cryptocurrency trade market has four major inherent forms of financial risks. They include:

Credit Risk

This impacts crypto operations. It revolves around the possibility of actors behind crypto projects erring in the execution of their expected duties (such as security or privacy). This risk is primarily associated with scams and thefts in the crypto world. A good instance is the hacking and breach of Binance in 2018, that resulted in the loss of more than $40 million worth of crypto assets.

Legal Risk

Legal risk relates to the likelihood of an unfavorable event happening as regards the set regulatory framework in a given jurisdiction. For example, an embargo on trading cryptocurrency in a particular country. A realistic instance of legal risk is when the government of Texas and North Carolina handed out a cease-and-desist order to the exchange of Bitconnect because of perceived fraud.

Liquidity Risk

Liquidity risk as regards crypto trading pertains to the probability of traders becoming incapable of converting their full position to fiat currencies (GBP, YEN, USD) which they can employ in their day-to-day expenditure.

Market Risk

This risk relates to the possibility of coin values going up or coming down different from your speculations in an open position.

Operational Risk

This risk is the likelihood that a crypto trader is not able to trade, put in funds, or remove money from their cryptocurrency wallets.

Major Risk Management Strategies

One of the biggest rules in crypto trading is: "Do not risk beyond what you can lose affordably." Considering the extent of risk involved in trading crypto, I normally advise crypto traders to utilize nothing over ten percent of their reserve or monthly income. Furthermore, trading with money that was borrowed is NEVER a wise option as it leaves you in a position of risk.

The strategies for the management of risk can be extensively classified into three:

- Risk/Reward Ratio

- Position-Sizing

- Stop Loss & Take Profits.

Risk/Reward Ratio

The risk/reward ratio relates to the real degree of risk with the possible returns. In trading, the riskier a position is, the more beneficial it can become. Interpreting the risk /reward ratio correctly allows you to realize when to join a trade and when it is wrong to do so.

Position Sizing

Position sizing decides the number of crypto coins or tokens a crypto trader is ready to buy. The odds of achieving amazing returns in crypto trading lures crypto traders to invest large percentages of their entire trading equity, even up to 100%. However, this is a wrong move that leaves you at the mercy of a drastic financial downturn. For emphasis, the rule here is that you should NEVER put all your eggs in one basket.

Stop Loss & Take Profits

Stop Loss is an order executed such that it completes an open position when a value declines to a certain boundary. While, Take Profits is an executable order that wipes out open orders when the value increases up to a particular point. Both are excellent strategies for managing risk. Stop Losses protect you from getting involved in unrewarding transactions, while Take Profits allow you to flee the trade before the market goes south and affects you.

You can bring in the services of Trailing Stop Losses and Take Profits which stick to the rate's shifts automatically. Such an effect still isn't accessible at most of the crypto exchanges. Thankfully, with terminals such as Superorder, you can fix your Trailing Stop Losses and Take Profits straight from the crypto terminal.

How To Cut The Losses And Stay Winning

Accept Losses

As I mentioned earlier, risk is an inevitable part of trading. In fact, we can't get rid of it. We can only learn to minimize the downside effects that come with these risks. You should, then, accept your failures (losses) and depend on strategy-based decisions and actions to achieve good returns in forthcoming trades.

Evaluate the Fees

Beginner traders most times do not recognize the kind of fees involved with trading. These fees include leverage fees, withdrawal fees, and so on. You should evaluate these fees in your strategy for managing risk.

Concentrate on the Success Rate

There will always be risks constantly present to deter you from trading. Despite this, concentrating on the number of times you succeed enables you to cultivate a positive mood in trading.

Assess Drawdown

This pertains to the entire decrease in your original funds following a string of downsides. For example, if you were to loss $2,000 from $6,000, your measure drawdown is 10%. The greater the sum, the more you would have to put into trading for it to recoup. I will advise that you retain a 6% risk threshold.

Risk management does not necessarily mean running away from risk or avoid trading due to the possibility of adverse results. Rather, efficient risk management is learning to cut your losses and stay winning. If you can learn to manage your risks when you trade, you will stay afloat.

Chapter 7

A Beginner's Guide to

Cryptocurrency Mining

"Over 80% of beginner traders believe they will never
need the knowledge of cryptocurrency mining until the
time comes, and they fall short!"
Anonymous

Inadequate knowledge of the workings of
cryptocurrency mining can leave you in shambles if you
dare attempt it without full information. You do not want
to be that beginner trader that falls short when the time
comes for him to utilize his understanding of
cryptocurrency mining. To not be that guy is to pay keen
attention to every nugget I will be sharing with you in
this chapter. By the end of this chapter, you should
already have all the knowledge required to handle
cryptocurrency competently and efficiently.

With cryptocurrencies gaining prominence and
hitting the everyday world with a bang, more people are

attracted to this sector. Of course, a lot of these new traders show interest in the crypto markets because they had heard that it is a good place to earn. Truly, mere owning a crypto asset can offer you earnings over a long period. But that's not the only way. In fact, that's not the best method to gain maximum profit from cryptocurrency.

The key to tapping maximum value from cryptocurrency is a trading method referred to as mining.

Understanding Cryptocurrency Mining

To explain this in the simplest possible words, cryptocurrency mining is a procedure in which a machine performs specific functions to gain a higher number of crypto coins. These functions are referred to as "Proof of Work". They are formulated to develop an even playing field for all the various miners out there mining cryptocurrency.

The functions themselves are simply math equations. The higher the number of miners aiming to mine from a certain mining pool, the more difficult the equations come to be. This creates a kind of balance in the mining pool. However, it again encourages bigger and greater machinery practice. Several additional underlying components come into play while the mining process is ongoing. But the common idea is that if your machine is a part of the mining process, you will get a percentage of the haul. That is a very brief and easy way of clarifying what cryptocurrency mining is. Now, let's proceed to what exactly you need to understand - how to mine cryptocurrency.

Cryptocurrency Mining: How Does It Work?

There are a few methods you could go about mining cryptocurrency. I will explain the major ones here and begin from the simplest of them all – cloud mining.

Cloud Mining

If you are searching for a way to go about mining cryptocurrency, cloud mining is perhaps the most prominent way to mine cryptocurrencies with very minimal digital activity. Cloud mining is a strategy that involves you paying someone (usually a big firm) a certain amount of money for them to "rent out" their mining machine (also known as a "rig"). This firm also handles the mining process.

This rent is for a fixed time span, within which all the income that the rig generates (aside from the electricity and maintenance expenses) goes into your cryptocurrency wallet.

The people firms that provide these cloud mining assistances often have big mining buildings with numerous farms for their usage. They likewise are well-grounded in the process of mining these cryptocurrencies. Cloud mining has evolved into a prominent practice primarily because it provides the chance to be a part of the world of cryptocurrencies even when you do not have sufficient funds to purchase your rigs. It also creates an opportunity for those who are not interested in owning a rig.

There are two ways to go about cloud mining. It can either be free or paid. Generally, a lot of people that are interested in mining cryptocurrency would lean towards the "free" alternative, but it does come with certain demerits. First, there is the issue of the slow mining pace and the absence of favorable mining conditions. On the other hand, paid cloud mining often works like this: You locate a cloud mining host on the internet. You evaluate the schemes that the host provides. Some hosts even furnish you with the means to generate and personalize your cloud mining scheme. Once you pick out what you are interested in, you merely have to pay the host, input your cryptocurrency wallet code. And that is how you begin the process of mining your own cryptocurrency!

CPU Mining

CPU mining makes use of computer processors for the cryptocurrency mining process. It used to be a workable alternative back in the early days of cryptocurrency adoption. However, over time, a few investors have opted for this mining technique. CPU mining is awfully slow. The process could go on for months without you getting the tiniest amount of earnings. It's likewise not often worth it. At the end of the day, you make only a little amount of cash, yet unfortunately, you spend ten times that sum on cooling and electricity.

Why then do people still even consider using CPU mining? Well, practically, it is because anyone that has a desktop computer can run the process. All you have to do is have sufficient knowledge of basic computer operations and specific software types. So, you don't have to outsource your cryptocurrency mining with all the potential uncertainties that come with it. You can be sure of the efforts being put into the mining process and own up to the results.

GPU Mining

GPU mining is perhaps the most famous cryptocurrency mining procedure among investors. If you run a search on Google for "cryptocurrency mining", GPU rigs are likely the first results you will get to see. The miners who received outsourced cryptocurrency for cloud mining, for instance, employ the services of GPU rigs for their process. No doubt, GPU miners are experts that often have hundreds, if not thousands, of rigs. So, it's safe to say that some level of safety is assured.

GPU mining is quite common due to its efficiency and somewhat inexpensive nature. However, the building of the rig itself is quite expensive. But when it gets to how fast the mining process is and the comprehensive work rate, the GPU mining rig is perfect.

GPU rigs make use of graphics cards to mine crypto coins. A typical rig comprises a motherboard, a processor, rig frame, cooling, and of course, several graphics cards. The standard price for a well-functioning and properly constructed GPU mining rig will likely be around the $3000 price spectrum. It is a huge investment but will yield returns even much faster than a CPU miner. People seeking ways to mine cryptocurrency should check out the GPU mining method.

ASIC Mining

ASICs (Application-Specific Integrated Circuits) are outstanding tools that are constructed exclusively to perform a sole function, which in this instance, is to mine cryptocurrency. ASICs are quite popular and cherished because they generate a lot of cryptocurrency compared to other methods (GPU and CPU). Yet, as amazing as this may sound, ASICs are a major topic of controversy.

When the ASIC firm declared a new version of the machine, there was an outcry in the cryptocurrency world. Most people had clamored for a total ban on these machines. Why? Because the ASICS are strong. They even deprive other miners who use GPU or CPU rigs of the chance to keep up in aspects of speed and how much they earn.

Furthermore, ASICs have shaken the economy of some cryptocurrencies. Imagine if the bulk of income would go to just one miner that has an ASIC farm. It will only result in chaos.

The Best Way To Mine Cryptocurrency

Now that you have enough knowledge on how to mine cryptocurrency, the next bone of contention becomes which mining technique you should adopt.

There is literally no hard and fast rule to the choice of cryptocurrency mining technique. Your selection of a method will boil down to how confidently you can answer these questions.

Are you ready to spend some money before making a profit? If yes, how much are you willing to spend?

Do you prefer to have your own rig? Or do you even want to make use of a rig to mine?

These and many more related questions will define the most favorable mining method for you. Though, GPU and cloud mining appear to be two major methods that investors prefer. CPU mining is sluggish and tiresome, while ASIC mining could become very erratic, especially given recent experiences.

If you prefer to construct your own rig, then GPU is the method for you. If you wouldn't like to spend any money and just get it underway immediately, you should consider CPU mining. But, if you're ready to take a chance and you're not scared of controversy, ASICs are a perfect way to mine. Summarily, cloud mining remains the best way to mine if you hope to avoid problems with rigs and other types of machinery.

Different Kinds Of Mining Software

CGMiner

This software is perhaps the most generally utilized software for cryptocurrency miners now (especially for Bitcoin miners). The software contains elements like CPU mining support, multi-GPU support, remote interface capabilities, fan speed control, and self-detection of new blocks.

BTCMiner

This Bitcoin software is established on an open-source forum. It comes with a USB interface and aided FPGA boards that can come in handy for communication and programming. It has numerous vital features, such as selecting the frequency that has the biggest rate of useful hashes. And because it is open source, it doesn't need a license for operation.

EasyMiner

This software operates on Android, Linux, and Windows systems. It has a striking user interface that is compatible with the CGminer software. The software is preferred because it generates simple visualization with graphs of your cryptocurrency mining explorations.

MulitMiner

This is another excellent visual interface, but this time, it is an interface for BFGMiner. This interface setup is very automatic, and it's a suitable fit for those who are new to cryptocurrency mining as it has an easy-to-use control panel.

Bitminer

Bitminer has been present for quite some time (since 2011), and it possesses many users. Its users are well over 450,000 in all. It also works well with GPU and CPU mining rigs, which are inexpensive to set up compared to ASIC type miners. Due to its flexibility, a lot of miners really relish using it.

RPC Miner

This is an exclusively MacOS compatible system that is best suited to miners who aren't conversant with Windows OS.

It Is Time To Start Mining

The cryptocurrency mining software you select is a relatively peculiar decision. The eventual result depends on the operating system you want to use and your choice of the visual user interface. Cryptocurrency mining can still be very productive, but like most other concepts, it requires resources, time, and a distinct skill set to go through the process.

Chapter 8

Developing the Right Mindset and Ethics

"I have been trading for decades, and I am still standing. I have seen a lot of traders come and go. They have a system or a program that works in some specific environments and fails in others. In contrast, my strategy is dynamic and ever evolving. I constantly learn and change."

Thomas Busby

Thomas Busby's remarks on the trading environment do not just show his wealth of experience but also how much he imbibes the right mindset and ethics. These are the tenets that make a successful trader. The same tenets you must hold dearly and reference as you forge ahead.

This is a primer for everyone who is new to cryptocurrency trading but is willing to see it through to the heights of success. This chapter is NOT aimed at providing investment advice. Instead, I will attempt to provide you with profitable tenets and signals to aid your journey from a beginner up to becoming a professional, successful crypto trader.

Here is a brief list of beliefs that are worth bearing in mind. They are the basic tenets of a successful trader.

Market Equilibrium

"For every action, there is an equal and opposite reaction."

Newton's Third Law of Motion

The crypto markets are constantly attempting to locate a point of equilibrium. Go through any chart, and you will discover that any swing in value, either a rise or a fall, is mostly confronted with a proportional and contrary swing in a different direction. This is one of the most valuable tenets to understand as a crypto trader Several crypto traders lose funds after getting tricked into playing catch up with the markets. They see the market value rising and decide to buy high. Shortly after, the price moves in the opposing direction. Understand how Newton's third law of motion applies to trading, and you will discover how traditional even the crypto markets can be.

Polarity

The basic idea behind equilibrium is a continual balance between opposite forces. The markets can only swing in two directions. And each exchange is a selection between buying or selling. Employ polarity to enable you to quantify the crypto market to make the favorable selection. Here's a list of polarities to enable you to interpret crypto market situations:

- High vs low

- Volatile vs stable

- Buying vs selling

- Good vs bad news

- Bull trend vs bear trend

- Healthy trend vs unhealthy trend

- Following the trend vs contrarian trading

- Support vs resistance

Cycles

The continual exchange between buying and selling generates voluntary cycles in the crypto markets. Most rises and falls happen with a string of huge spikes. Then you will have retracement (short-term price change), choppiness (being stuck in a price range for long) and eventually consolidation (higher transfer fees). Understanding the tempo of price movement will enable you to time the markets and foresee prospects for forthcoming developments.

Develop an Adaptable Framework

"When the wind blows, the grass bends."
Confucius

Let's put aside complicated trade inquiry to simplify price movement into its easiest form. Apart from a diagonal crypto market, there are two main directions a market can move, up or down. Without considering all the variables, any exchange can offer you a 50/50 chance. Most crypto traders become hell-bent on holding a hard position and leaping to one side or the other. A flexible trader will consider both likelihoods and react based on what the market poses.

Crypto trading is not just about nice charts and being precise; it is about earning money. Occasionally your calculation of the markets is incorrect, and you may find yourself on the bad side of an exchange. Do you rigidly clench onto your old notions, or do you let that pass and adjust to the circumstance as it presents itself? That's some trading character check you should consider.

There is a thin line between being flexible and playing catch-up with the markets. At times, it makes more sense to keep up with the course and not get intimidated out of healthy trade.

Equilibrium is the sole requirement for successful trading. How long can you change positions with the trend of the markets without losing equilibrium and getting into a loss? Can you conform to a quick turn without getting thrown off balance? To maintain your equilibrium in crypto trading, you must constantly watch both sides of the divide. Generate a strategy that can adjust to both likely results of the markets, whether it goes up or come down. Always keep an exit plan for both winning and losing exchanges.

The 1 Kick Tactic

"I fear not the man who's practiced 10,000 kicks once, but I fear the man who has practiced one kick 10,000 times."
Bruce Lee

There are several ways to make money when you trade in the crypto markets. Possibly, you may employ a lot of them as a hybrid when you see the chance. That said, there is one way to stand out among the others and help you achieve those constant returns. Productive trading isn't about possessing a hundred fancy tactics: it is about your earnings. The more constant your returns are, the better it becomes for you. Traders who strive for the highest possible returns despite the huge risk will possibly lose money. Instead of that, discover a stable structure and strategy to capitalize on the market.

Quality Over Quantity

Don't spend your time aimlessly believing you constantly have to be in an exchange or another. Quality over quantity is important to be an active trader. There are certain market situations that furnish you with an earning likelihood that's more than 50/50. By utilizing the tenets of equilibrium, you will begin to understand what patterns can bend the likelihoods to your advantage. A disciplined crypto trader is like a tiger patiently stalking its prey. Realize when to function and when to stay still and do nothing!

Other ideas that would help you become the best you can be and make the most of the markets include:

- Avoid trading based on your emotions

- Understand and make use of risk management

- Know and employ technical analysis

- Understand the big distinction between fundamental analysis and technical analysis. That way, you can know which is applicable in various market situations.

- Learn to take out your profits when you are in a winning position.

Interesting to say that every single knowledge you have gained in the pages of this treasured guide is best understood in practice. And as you must already know, there is no route to free money unless you expend efforts, regardless of how little. If there is one parting fact, it's as obvious as day that a cryptocurrency is a dependable form of investment. Call it money-doubling if you would, but asides from the possibility of volatile bear markets, you can recoup generational profits by investing in crypto assets.

The knowledge you've gained won't trade itself, you know. So, if you feel up to the task already, why not pick out a productive cryptocurrency and sow a seed reasonably. Digital assets are a treasure worth digging for. So, dig. All you've got to lose is your fears and mediocrity.

With that, I officially welcome you to the world of blockchain technology and cryptocurrency!

Disclaimer

This book contains opinions and ideas of the author and is meant to teach the reader informative and helpful knowledge while due care should be taken by the user in the application of the information provided. The instructions and strategies are possibly not right for every reader and there is no guarantee that they work for everyone. Using this book and implementing the information/recipes therein contained is explicitly your own responsibility and risk. This work with all its contents, does not guarantee correctness, completion, quality or correctness of the provided information. Misinformation or misprints cannot be completely eliminated.

Printed in Great Britain
by Amazon